THIS IS HISTORY!

Dying for the Vote

HOW ORDINARY PEOPLE WON THE RIGHT TO VOTE

JANE
RICHARDSON

IAN
DAWSON

WITHDRAWN

JOHN MURRAY

The Schools History Project

The Project was set up in 1972, with the aim of improving the study of history for students aged 13–16. This involved a reconsideration of the ways in which history contributes to the educational needs of young people. The Project devised new objectives, new criteria for planning and developing courses, and the materials to support them. New examinations, requiring new methods of assessment, also had to be developed. These have continued to be popular. The advent of GCSE in 1987 led to the expansion of Project approaches into other syllabuses.

The Schools History Project has been based at Trinity and All Saints College, Leeds, since 1978, from where it supports teachers through a biennial Bulletin, regular INSET, an annual conference and a website (www.tasc.ac.uk/shp).

Since the National Curriculum was drawn up in 1991, the Project has continued to expand its publications, bringing its ideas to courses for Key Stage 3 as well as a range of GCSE and A level specifications.

Words printed in SMALL CAPITALS are defined in the Glossary on page 68.

© Jane Richardson and Ian Dawson 2002

First published in 2002
by John Murray (Publishers) Ltd
50 Albemarle Street
London W1S 4BD

Layouts by Amanda Hawkes
Artwork by Neil Chapman, Richard Duszczak, Janek Matysiak, Tony Randell, Edward Ripley, Steve Smith
Typeset in 13/15pt Goudy by Wearset Ltd, Boldon, Tyne and Wear
Printed and bound in Spain by Bookprint, S.L., Barcelona

A catalogue entry for this book is available from the British Library

Pupils' Book ISBN 0 7195 8563 5
Teachers' Resource Book ISBN 0 7195 8564 3

◆ Contents

Can you persuade the couch potatoes to vote?

◆ Can you persuade them to vote?

> When I'm old enough, I'll be the first one to vote. We've been studying how people fought – and died – for the right to vote.

> Maybe if our parents knew what working people went through to win the right to vote they would take it more seriously.

Your advertising campaign starts here

Your task will be to create an advertising campaign to help persuade the couch potatoes to vote. The campaign will be called 'Voting Matters'. It will use lessons from history plus your own ideas to persuade ordinary people to vote.

For your campaign you will create:

◆ three large **posters** to go on buses, bus shelters or other poster sites
◆ a four-page **leaflet** to be delivered to people's homes
◆ a storyboard for a **TV advertisement** to be screened at peak time.

Discuss

Throughout Section 1 you will be investigating the following questions.

1 Why did people want the vote?
2 What methods did people use to try to win the vote?
3 How successful were their methods?

4 Why did people die trying to win the right to vote?

Using the timeline that your teacher will give you, discuss each of these questions and work out some first answers. As you work through the section you will find out if your first ideas need revising.

Midnight, 3 November 1839. In the coal-black, ice-frozen hills above the town of Newport in Wales, men and women gathered in their thousands. Their breath creating silvery clouds in the night air, they stamped and shivered but they shivered with excitement, not cold. The people were on the march! They wanted the vote, the first step to improving their lives at work and at home.

At dawn they marched down into Newport, PIKES, MUSKETS and clubs at the ready, to take control of the town and release people who had been imprisoned after earlier protests. They believed this would force the government to give them the vote.

Soldiers were waiting in the centre of Newport. Fire! A volley of shots ripped into the crowd, then another volley, then another. About twenty men died that morning. Another hundred were arrested and the leaders were transported for life to the prison colonies in Australia.

In this section of the book you are going to investigate why people like those in Newport died for the vote in the 1800s . . . and whether it did any good.

WHY DID PEOPLE DIE FOR THE VOTE IN THE 1800s...

and did it do any good?

"My name is Feargus O'Connor. I'm going to show you why working people are angry. By working people I mean people who don't have much money, who have to work hard for a living. There are three big reasons."

◆ Reason 1: Working people did not have the right to vote

"The first reason is that working people don't have the right to vote. Only the rich can vote. And the way they vote is so unfair, as you can see in the picture opposite.

MPs are not paid so only the rich can be Members of Parliament. Working people cannot afford to become MPs. That means there are no working people in Parliament to speak up about the changes we need.

The cities where working people live don't even have MPs. The CONSTITUENCIES have hardly changed for 400 years. Manchester, Leeds and Bradford are all rich, important cities but none of them sends an MP to Parliament. Yet the village of Dunwich still has an MP and it fell into the sea hundreds of years ago!"

ACTIVITY

1 Look at the picture opposite. It shows an election in 1830. Find out how people vote in elections today. What are the differences between voting in 1830 and voting today?
2 How are the voters in 1830 (people in colour) different from the rest of the people?
3 Why would it be easy to bribe voters in the 1830s?
4 Look at O'Connor's main criticisms. Draw up a list of changes that would make the voting system fairer.
5 Construct a timeline to show the main events in the 1800s as working men fought for the right to vote. Your teacher can give you a sheet with some dates to start you off. You can add to the timeline as you work through Section 1.

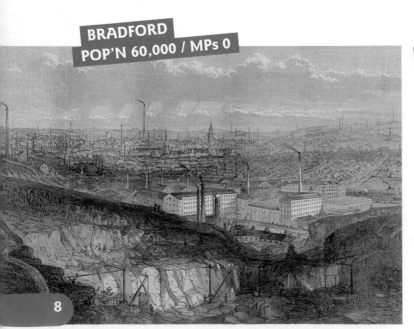

BRADFORD
POP'N 60,000 / MPs 0

DUNWICH
POP'N 0 / MPs 1

AN ELECTION IN 1830

◆ *Reason 2: Living conditions were awful*

"This is Leeds. People move here to work in the factories. They have to live close to their work. So lots of houses have been built right next to the factories."

Houses have been built cheaply in rows called 'back-to-backs'. There are usually twenty or so houses in a terrace. Lots of families can be crammed in.

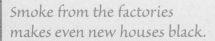

Smoke from the factories makes even new houses black.

The smell is indescribable! The gutter should take rain-water away but most of the time it overflows with stale water.

Rubbish piles high. Landlords don't get rid of the rubbish so the rats make it their home – and the children play here.

Look at the queue for the stand-pipe! Those at the back might not be lucky – it's only on for 30 minutes. The rest will take their buckets to the stream. All the water round here tastes foul, not surprising if you see the rubbish that goes in it.

Euh! The smell in here is no better. The whole family of eight is at home. The family sleep, eat and cook together in this room. As you can see there isn't much furniture. The family share the bed and the bed bugs too! Everyone is kept awake at night with the children's coughing. It's not surprising with that damp running down the walls.

Children take turns to get warm by the fire. The meal is cooked in the pot. These houses don't have kitchens.

The walls are black with damp. The builder was too interested in making money to do anything about making the house waterproof. There are no laws controlling how these houses are built.

ACTIVITY

1 List all the things that O'Connor thinks are wrong with living conditions in Leeds.
2 Living conditions were so unhealthy that the average life expectancy for the poor in Leeds was eighteen years. Explain how these conditions could lead to people dying young.
3 Make a list of changes that might help improve living conditions.
4 Can you work out why having the right to vote might help these people? Write a sentence about this.

◆ *Reason 3: Working conditions were hard*

"Now I'll show you where people work and how hard they work. First, we'll have a look inside a cotton mill in Lancashire. The mill owner is very rich indeed. His mill is well built compared to the workers' houses. It has strong brick walls and windows to let in the light."

FACTORY RULES

1. Any person late when the engine starts shall be fined 3d.
2. Any person who leaves the room without permission shall be fined 3d.
3. All broken brushes, oilcans, windows &c. shall be paid for by the worker.
4. Any person found talking shall be fined 2d.
5. For every Oath or bad language, 3d for the first offence, and if repeated they shall be dismissed.
6. Any person wilfully damaging this Notice shall be dismissed.

The mill is kept hot and damp to stop the cotton threads from breaking. This is good for cotton but tiring for the workers themselves.

The working day starts at five o'clock and doesn't finish until seven at night. There are no limits on the hours anyone works. People are calling for a Ten Hours Act – no one should be forced to work more than ten hours a day.

Many of the workers here are children. They are cheap to employ and easy to control. The overseer beats them with his belt if he thinks they are slacking.

Children sweep up the dust which makes them cough a lot. Small children crawl under the machines to collect waste or fix the machines, even though the machines are still working.

"Not everyone works in a factory. This family makes nails in a noisy, hot hut attached to their small cottage in Sedgley near Birmingham."

This family can work when they like. They don't have to start and finish at set times like workers in the mills and mines. Instead they have a target of producing 10,000 nails in a week.

A nail master delivers bars of iron at the beginning of the week, then the family must make the nails by the end of the week when the nails are weighed, collected and the man of the family is paid.

It's a tiring sixteen-hour day. Tempers as well as sparks are flying by Saturday! The children know not to get in the way.

Children from five years old must work. They keep the fire going or help make the nails. There are many accidents with so many in such a small space.

Sunday is a rest day but most nail makers also have Monday off as well. They call it Saint Monday. The man of the family sleeps off his Sunday night's drink. The mother and oldest children do the washing in the tub in the main room.

ACTIVITY

1. Choose one of the workers shown on these two pages. Explain what his/her job is and what they might like or dislike about it.
2. Explain how the work might affect the worker's health.
3. Make a list of new laws that might help improve working conditions.
4. Why might the right to vote help these people?

◆ How did people try to win the vote?

Many people believed that if they could win the right to vote then they would be able to improve their living and working conditions. So the campaign for the vote was also a campaign to improve their lives.

In the early 1800s, there were many campaigns to win the right to vote.

ACTIVITY A

1 Captions A, B and C below tell you about three protests. Which caption fits Source 1?

A In 1817, men from Manchester set out to march to London with only a blanket each and some food. They went to hand in their petition demanding the right to vote. The marchers were soon turned back by soldiers.

B In 1819, the army killed eleven people who were taking part in a meeting to demand the vote at St Peter's Fields, Manchester. This was called the Peterloo massacre.

C In 1830, farmworkers set fire to hay ricks in protest against new machinery which could put them out of work. Many were arrested and some were transported to Australia.

2 How can you tell from all three captions that the government was afraid of protests?

3 None of these protests succeeded. Do you think this made people more or less determined to win the vote?

SOURCE 1

ACTIVITY B

Feargus O'Connor was a brilliant speaker. He could whip a crowd into a frenzy. See if you can help him to write a paragraph for a speech to convince his listeners that working people should have the vote. Choose one of these topics and write a paragraph of persuasive speech:

a) What's wrong with the voting system?

b) What's wrong with living conditions?

c) What's wrong with working conditions?

Keep to the facts but make sure your listeners really feel that the system is unfair. If you are really keen you could write about all three problems but for a good speech it is better to make the most of one point than to spread your speech too thinly over three points.

Source 2 is a good example of persuasive writing.

1 The passage is full of strong, emotive verbs and adjectives which are supposed to persuade the reader that the crowd were fair, ordinary people. Two are in **bold**. These words make us feel sympathetic towards the crowd. Can you spot any more loaded words that have been used in Source 2?

2 A rhetorical question is <u>underlined</u>. This question does not need an answer; it is used for effect. Think about the effect it has on us as readers. How does this work?

3 A short, sharp phrase ends the first paragraph. Why is this effective?

SOURCE 2 This passage was written by Samuel Bamford, one of the protesters who witnessed the Peterloo massacre. He wanted to make sure his readers sympathised with the protesters and not with the government.

*Sixty thousand **innocent** men, women and children gathered tightly together in St. Peter's Fields, Manchester in August 1819. They were **suffering** from extremely high unemployment and steep increases in the cost of bread. All they wanted was lower food prices to feed their starving families and to vote in elections. <u>Was this not reasonable and fair?</u> The great speaker Henry Hunt was to address the peaceful crowd. The government, however, was not in a mood for peace.*

The SABRES glistened in the air and on they went direct for the hustings [platform]. As the cavalry approached ... sabres were plied to hew a way through naked held up hands and defenceless heads; and then chopped limbs and wound-gaping skulls were seen and groans and cries were mingled with that din of that horrid confusion. Several mounds of human beings still remained where they had fallen, crushed down and smothered.

◆ 1831: Was Britain on the edge of revolution?

The politicians were afraid of revolution. In 1789 a revolution had started in France. The King, Queen and many nobles had been executed but so had many ordinary people. Anyone suspected of going against the revolution was sent to the guillotine: 17,000 people were executed! The government in Britain did not want that to happen to them. They thought revolution would bring disaster for everybody.

However, by 1831 food prices and unemployment were rising again. There were protest meetings all over the country. Some meetings turned into riots. This is what happened:

We have stormed Nottingham Castle, the home of the Duke of Newcastle, and the houses of others who are against reforms. The Duke influences the elections by BRIBING and threatening voters. If anyone dares to vote against his wishes he turns their families out onto the streets. The soldiers tried to stop us and they've taken many prisoners. Those poor souls will be sentenced to death or TRANSPORTATION just for wanting the vote!

SOURCE 3 In Bristol, rioters smashed windows, burned down the city jail and many other houses. Soldiers were sent in to restore order. Twelve men were killed and over a hundred were wounded.

The Duke of Wellington had been a great hero in 1815 when he beat Napoleon Bonaparte at the Battle of Waterloo. However, in 1831 he believed that giving more people the vote would lead to more and more reforms that would ruin the country, cause civil war and lead to disaster for everybody. So he was one of the leaders of the House of Lords who refused to give more people the vote. That was why crowds stoned his London house in 1831 and chanted 'Bonaparte for ever'. A mob even threatened to drag him off his horse until soldiers gave him an escort.

Riots continued. A rumour spread that 200,000 protesters were planning to march from Birmingham to London. It was said that they would not leave London until Parliament agreed to more people having the vote. The government ordered a regiment of soldiers to 'rough-sharpen' their sabres to stop the march but the soldiers refused to obey!

This really frightened the Prime Minister and his government. They thought that a revolution was about to break out. This wasn't surprising. They had just received an anonymous letter saying:

'Depend upon it the country is ripe for revolution . . . then goodbye to England's King and Ministers!'

What should they do?

SOURCE 4 Wellington looks out of his windows, broken by rioters. A drawing from 1833.

> There is a real danger of revolution. We must make some changes but I am **totally against** every man having the vote. Only respectable, educated men who own land should be able to vote.

> We should give middle-class men such as factory owners the vote and allow some northern towns such as Manchester, Leeds and Bradford to have a few MPs. That will make the factory owners happy and stop them leading protests.

> People who own land and wealth are the only ones intelligent enough to vote. But even some of them, the middle classes in towns, cannot vote. We must allow rich middle-class men in our towns to vote – and let them be MPs as well.

ACTIVITY

1 What would you advise the Prime Minister to do? Think about each option below, then write the Prime Minister a note explaining which option you think would be the best and why your choice is better than the other options.

   a) Give middle-class men the vote.

   b) Give all men over 21 the vote.

   c) Give the vote to all men and women over 21.

   d) Keep voting only for the very rich and deal harshly with all protesters.

2 Make a list of the different types of protest in 1831.

3 How did the government try to stop these protests?

WOULD YOU JOIN THE CHARTISTS?

In June 1832, the House of Lords finally gave in and passed the Reform Act. The picture below shows an election scene in 1835. What has changed?

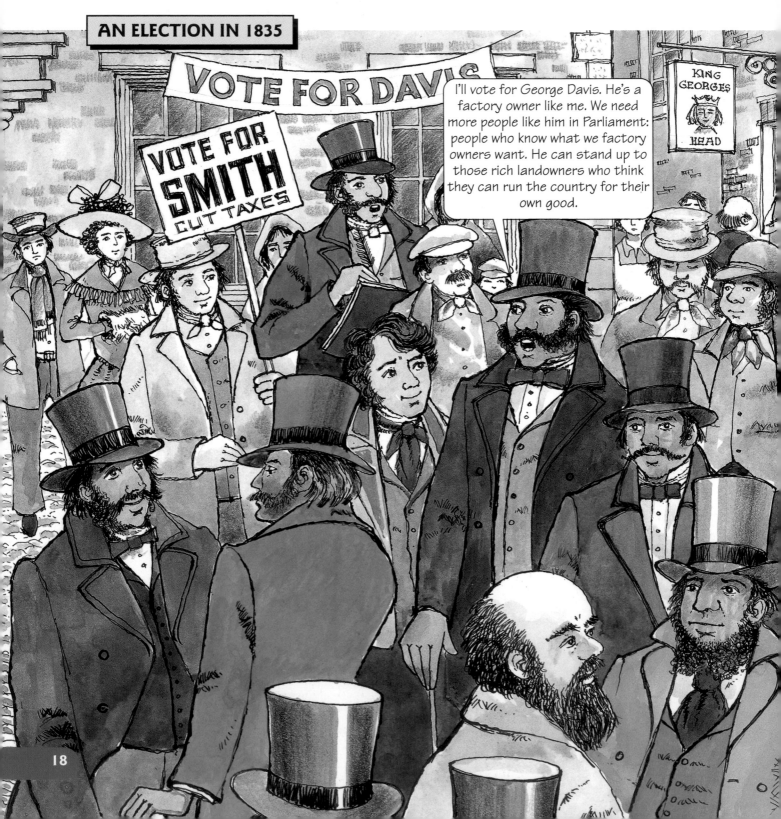

AN ELECTION IN 1835

Charles Dickens (who later became a famous novelist) was working as a newspaper reporter in 1835. This is how he described an election in that year:

> The noise and confusion here this morning is so great that my head is spinning. There are about forty flags on either side, two tremendous bands and 150 constables . . . The voters are drinking and guzzling and howling and roaring in every house of entertainment there is.

The Reform Act

The Reform Act increased the number of men who could vote from one in ten to two in ten.

But . . .

- Voters still had to own property or land – so only middle-class people could vote.
- Working people (those who did not own property) still could not vote.
- Voters still had to be men.
- Voting was still in public, so everyone could see who a person was voting for.
- Bribery and fear were still a big part in elections.

The other big change they made was that cities like Leeds, Manchester and Bradford all got MPs for the first time.

But . . .

- Most MPs were still from the South of England and from the countryside.

ACTIVITY

Compare the picture and information on page 18 with the similar picture on page 9.

1 On your own copy of the 1835 picture mark what has changed since 1830.
2 For each change write a sentence to explain it.
3 Write a third sentence to explain what has not changed.

What happened next?

If you went for option **a)** in Activity 1 on page 17 then the government would have been very pleased with you. That's what they chose too. They gave middle-class men the right to vote for the first time. But that did not meet the demands of the working men. The working people who had been part of the campaign felt betrayed. They'd given energy, enthusiasm and skill to the campaign but had got nothing. Only the middle classes had benefited. And to make matters worse, it was those middle classes who then brought in one of the most unpopular new laws of all.

◆ *Workhouses for the poor – another reason to riot!*

Nowadays the government helps anyone who is unemployed, disabled, old or sick and off work for a long time. In 1830 this was up to the local parish council. Money called the Poor Rate was collected from better-off people and given to the poor.

In 1832 this system was in crisis. More people were unemployed so the cost was rising. The middle classes were paying higher poor rates. These same middle-class people were also the 'new' voters and they put pressure on their MPs to do something about this. The government came up with a solution to this problem – a new Poor Law. The key feature of this was the workhouse.

We should stop the poor receiving money while they live at home. They should only get help if they move into a workhouse and the workhouse conditions should be so bad that only the really helpless people will ask for help. They'll feel like criminals! Workhouses will put people off being poor. That will cut the costs. Poor people are well able to help themselves. Giving them money just makes them scroungers.

1 Stable or other purposes.
2 Washouse.
3 Laundry.
4 Potatoes.
5 Relief-Stores.
6 Bread, Bacon, &c.
7 Porter.
8 Bakehouse.
9 Men's Day-Room.
10 Workroom.
11 Refractory Ward.
12 Dead-House.
13 Refractory Ward.
14 Passage.

SCALE OF FEET

SOURCE 1 Plan of a model workhouse.

Why did people hate the workhouse so much?

Anti-Poor Law Associations were formed. Around 100,000 people signed a petition asking the government to get rid of the Poor Law. Then riots broke out in many towns and cities, particularly in the North of England. Riots delayed the building of many workhouses for four years. See if you can work out what people hated so much.

SOURCE 2 Regulations for running the workhouses issued in 1835.

WORKHOUSE REGULATIONS

1. The Poor person shall be thoroughly cleansed and clothed in workhouse uniform. Personal possessions will be taken from him.
2. Poor people will be separated by sex on entering the workhouse.
3. A mother or father will be allowed an interview with their child once a day.

SOURCE 3

PUNISHMENT GUIDELINES

The following are offences to be punished:
1. Making a noise when silence is ordered including at mealtimes.
2. Refusing to work.
3. Pretending to be sick.
4. Using bad language.
5. Playing cards.
6. Climbing over the boundary wall.

Paupers found committing any of these offences will be given only bread and potatoes for two days.

SOURCE 4

RECOMMENDED DIET IN THE WORKHOUSE

Breakfast—6oz. bread, 1½ pints gruel
Dinner—1½ pints soup
Supper—6oz. bread, 2oz. cheese

SOURCE 5 Mrs Grasby speaking to an anti-Poor Law meeting in Elland, Yorkshire on 17 February 1838. This followed an anti-workhouse riot. The women went and rolled the workhouse Guardians in the snow.

Women have more to do with this cruel measure than men. The pain of being separated from those to whom we have looked for support, and from the children of our own bearing are more severe than it is possible for men to feel.

ACTIVITY

1 Look at Source 1. What does the plan show about the way families were to be split up?
2 Compare the Women's Yard and the Men's Yard. What does the plan tell you about the different work the men and women were expected to do in the workhouse?
3 Study the rest of the information on these two pages and, working with a partner, make a list of all the reasons why you think a poor person would hate the workhouse.

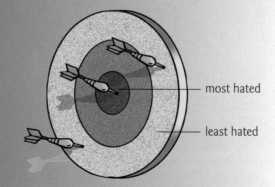

most hated

least hated

4 Make your own very large copy of a target then fill it in from the 'hate list' you have drawn up for question 3. In the centre write what you think would be most hated; in the outer circle the least hated. In the middle circle put the rest.
5 Choose one thing you have put in the centre circle and write a paragraph to explain why you chose that order. For example, I think the most hated thing about the workhouse system was . . . because . . . To me this was worse than . . . because . . .

21

◆ Would you join the Chartists?

It should be clear to you by now that the working people felt angry about lots of things in the 1830s. Out of this anger a new movement appeared – CHARTISM, led by Feargus O'Connor. Remember, at this time, people were campaigning for all **men** to have the vote. Getting women the vote was not yet an issue.

> And they've still done nothing about living conditions. Unless we get working men as MPs our living conditions will never improve. These rich MPs don't know what it's like to live in houses only fit for animals – and to see whole families wiped out by disease. If we can't vote there's no reason they should try to help us, is there?

> There's still no working men in Parliament. We make this country wealthy. We make the cloth and the ships. We mine the coal and iron. There should be working men in Parliament to represent us.

> We've been betrayed by the middle classes. We went to their meetings and rallies. We marched. We signed PETITIONS. But only the factory owners and the bankers got the vote in '32.

MARY ANN

FRANK

WILLIAM

GEORGE

JANE

> And instead of helping us when times are hard they have forced through a humiliating new Poor Law to save them money. How can we get rid of this new Poor Law? Riots can stop them building a workhouse but we can't get rid of the law until we have MPs that support our point of view.

> And they've still done nothing about working hours. If we could vote we would force them to pass a 'Ten Hours Act'. No working man should be forced to work more than ten hours a day. Parliament made slavery illegal. They should also do something about the white slaves in the TEXTILE mills of Yorkshire.

REPEAL

THE VOTE FOR EVERYMAN

READ THE TRUTH IN THE NORTHERN STAR

SECRET BALLOT

REPEAL THE POOR LAW

It all depends on the vote. The vote gives us power to change everything. Why should only the rich make the laws? Why should you go hungry in a land of plenty? Aren't you equal in the eyes of God to the man who employs you? Why of course you are, my friends! But without the vote you are powerless. With the vote you are powerful. So if you want change, sign this Charter. Join the Chartists . . .

FEARGUS O'CONNOR

The Six Points
OF THE
PEOPLE'S
CHARTER.

1. A VOTE for every man twenty-one years of age, of sound mind, and not undergoing punishment for crime.
2. THE BALLOT.—To protect the elector in the exercise of his vote.
3. NO PROPERTY QUALIFICATION for Members of Parliament—thus enabling the constituencies to return the man of their choice, be he rich or poor.
4. PAYMENT OF MEMBERS, thus enabling an honest tradesman, working man, or other person, to serve a constituency, when taken from his business to attend to the interests of the country.
5. EQUAL CONSTITUENCIES, securing the same amount of representation for the same number of electors, instead of allowing small constituencies to swamp the votes of large ones.
6. ANNUAL PARLIAMENTS, thus presenting the most effectual check to bribery and intimidation, since though a constituency might be bought once in every seven years (even with the ballot), no purse could buy a constituency (under a system of universal suffrage) in each ensuing twelvemonth; and since members, when elected for a year only, would not be able to defy and betray their constituents as now.

SOURCE 6 The Six Points of the People's Charter. The ballot means a secret rather than a public vote.

ACTIVITY

1 **a)** Summarise each speaker's grievances on a separate piece of card. Don't re-write the whole thing, just give a heading and a brief explanation.
   b) On a large sheet of paper sort the grievances into two groups: politics on one side and living standards on the other.
   c) Paste them on to the paper, keeping to the two groups.
2 Think about the way these grievances are connected. Draw lines and add labels to show the connections.
3 Choose one speaker on this page and write a paragraph explaining why you think this person would have joined the Chartists in 1838.

In 1838 working people had four options to get more power:

1. Start a revolution like people had done in France in 1789.
2. Riot as they had done in England seven years earlier in 1831.
3. Send a petition to Parliament asking for the People's Charter to be made law.
4. Do nothing and avoid all the trouble.

Most people decided that option 3, the peaceful petitioning of Parliament, was their best choice. All over the country men and women joined Chartist groups. There were over 80 women's Chartist groups alone. They believed that the Charter's Six Points would make Britain a better and fairer place to live. First, they had to get millions of people to sign a petition for the Charter, and take it to Parliament. What happened next?

1 The first petition won masses of support

"MPs can't ignore the voices of 1.2 million people can they?"

"There will be trouble if they do."

May 1839. The petition was signed by 1.2 million people but it was rejected by 235 votes to 46 in Parliament.

2 Chartists arrested! Soldiers sent north!

The Trumpet

BIRMINGHAM CHARTISTS ARRESTED IN CLASHES WITH POLICE!!

In July 1839, soldiers and police clashed with peaceful Chartist protesters in Birmingham. Chartists were arrested and 6000 soldiers were sent to the North in case of more protests.

5 1842 Second Chartist petition was rejected

Spring 1842. All over Britain wages were cut by 25 per cent. Unemployment rose and the workhouses were overflowing. Three million people signed the new Chartist petition. The petition was rejected – again!

6 The protests began again

When the Charter was rejected, 50,000 people went on strike in and around Manchester. Soon the strikers marched over the Pennines to Yorkshire. The government ordered soldiers to be sent by railway to keep order.

ACTIVITY

Get into groups of four. It is September 1842. Two of you are Chartists and two of you are leaders of the Tory government.

1 Discuss and note down how you are feeling after the events of 1839–42, e.g. angry, upset, worried, fearful, determined. Give examples of recent events that have made you feel like this.

2 In your pairs do either Activity **a)** OR **b)**.

   a) Why did you, as government leaders, decide to:

    ◆ transport or jail Chartists
    ◆ ban nearly all meetings

    ◆ use spies to report on Chartist meetings
    ◆ not change the Poor Law?

b) As Chartists, what would you do now? Give reasons for your choice.

    ◆ Riot.
    ◆ Organise another petition.
    ◆ Find other ways to build up support.
    ◆ Forget it all and go home.

3 Tell your 'opposite' pair what you have chosen and how you feel. Do you see their point of view? If not, why not?

3 Newport rising 1839

Seven thousand miners and ironworkers marched into Newport. They planned to capture important towns. Soldiers killed twenty protesters and arrested another 100. The leaders were transported to Australia for life.

4 Chartists sent to jail

I sentence you to eighteen months in jail.

Spring 1840. Over 500 Chartists were sent to jail including O'Connor. More protests took place, especially in Yorkshire. There was a great Chartist procession to celebrate O'Connor's release.

7 Fighting for the vote

We won't go home. You can kill us if you like!

Soldiers tried to stop the strikers joining together across the North. Shots were fired. The crowds clashed with the troops but the soldiers won control. Strikers were arrested and sent to York Castle for questioning.

8 The end of the protests

The mills began work again. Many strikers were released as long as they kept the peace, but ten were jailed. The magistrates said 'We have taught a good many that the arm of the law was stronger than they.'

◆ Two views of 1848 – did the Chartists plan a revolution?

After the strikes of 1842 the country was peaceful. The Chartists saw the pressure pay off. In 1847, Parliament introduced the Ten Hours Act – limiting working hours in textile mills to ten hours per day. But in 1848 the Chartists were back.

1848 according to Wellington: Revolution foiled!

"In 1848, the Chartists caused trouble again. They said it was because of unemployment and high food prices. In Glasgow unemployed workers shouted 'Bread or Revolution'. They had heard about the revolutions all over Europe. Then they organised another petition and a huge meeting.

They said their petition had over 5 million signatures but many of them were forgeries. They even forged the Queen's signature – and mine!

I could not take the chance of them attacking Parliament and starting a revolution. So, as commander-in-chief of the British army, I took the following precautions:

◆ I sent Queen Victoria to her palace on the Isle of Wight for safety.
◆ The Bank of England and the Post Office were barricaded.
◆ We placed cannon on London's bridges in case the Chartists tried to attack Parliament.
◆ Around 85,000 special constables were sworn in. All kinds of people became specials, from city bankers to household servants.
◆ And just in case, we had 4000 police and 8000 soldiers standing by!

And it worked! They delivered their petition but did not dare try any violence. By 2p.m. the Prime Minister wrote to the Queen that all was safe. We had saved London from revolution!"

SOURCE 1 Thousands of people joined the Chartist demonstration on Kennington Common, London, 10 April 1848. This is one of the very earliest news photographs.

1848 according to O'Connor: Petition delivered!

"We never meant to start a revolution! Thousands joined the Chartists because they were desperate. Food prices had risen steeply. People lost their jobs because factories were losing orders.

So many people signed our petition that it had to be carried in a series of horse-drawn coaches! Wellington says that lots of the names were forgeries but that's unfair. Many people could not write so they simply copied the writing of someone else. It was the only way they could show they supported the Charter.

We went to London to hold a peaceful rally. The government was worried because of the revolutions abroad but we did not want violence either. All those cannon and police were unnecessary. And many of those special constables were forced to join up by their employers – or lose their jobs!

We were partly successful. We handed in our petition and we showed how much support we had. We also showed how working-class people could behave sensibly in our campaign for the vote. But we still failed to win the vote. The government still would not let ordinary men have the vote."

CHARTIST DEMONSTRATION!!

"PEACE and ORDER" is our MOTTO!

TO THE WORKING MEN OF LONDON.

Fellow Men,—The Press having misrepresented and vilified us and our intentions, the Demonstration Committee therefore consider it to be their duty to state that the grievances of us (the Working Classes) are deep and our demands just. We and our families are pining in misery, want, and starvation! We demand a fair day's wages for a fair day's work! We are the slaves of capital—we demand protection to our labour. We are political serfs—we demand to be free. We therefore invite all well disposed to join in our peaceful procession on

MONDAY NEXT, April 10,

As it is for the good of all that we seek to remove the evils under which we groan.

The following are the places of Meeting of THE CHARTISTS, THE TRADES, THE IRISH CONFEDERATE & REPEAL BODIES:

East Division on Stepney Green at 8 o'clock; **City and Finsbury Division** on Clerkenwell Green at 9 o'clock; **West Division** in Russell Square at 9 o'clock; and the **South Division** in Peckham Fields at 9 o'clock, and proceed from thence to Kennington Common.

Signed on behalf of the Committee, JOHN ARNOTT, Sec.

DISCUSS

Which of these viewpoints do you most agree with?

a) The Chartists wanted to start a revolution in 1848 but the government was so well organised it stopped them.

b) The Chartists did not plan a revolution in 1848. They wanted to deliver their petition peacefully.

Find evidence from these two pages to support your choice.

◆ Success at last

Working people did not win the vote in 1848. So in that sense Chartism failed. But Chartism was part of a much bigger movement that continued through the next twenty years until 1867, when there was the first really major breakthrough. You can see how this happened through the story of Joseph Taylor, a former Chartist.

How did Joseph Taylor win the right to vote in 1867?

After 1848 there were no more Chartist petitions and very few riots or strikes. Britain was in a boom. Industry did well. Wages were rising. Workers were better off.

Chartism disappeared. But the people who had run Chartism did not disappear. Their desire for the vote did not disappear either. People like Joseph Taylor put their energy into other ways of improving their lives. Joseph taught in a school. Others got themselves educated. They felt that was a surer way to improve their lives than petitions or strikes.

But they had not lost their desire for the vote. For many of them it was as strong as ever. One writer described the country's workers in 1861 as 'Almost to a man these workers are red-hot politicians – with a sense of their importance in the State of Britain.'

Slowly but surely MPs in Parliament began to adjust to the idea that working men had earned the right to vote. Many said they were impressed by the fact that nearly all the protests for the vote were now peaceful. They were also impressed by the way working people worked hard to educate themselves and improve their own situation.

In 1866 Parliament debated a bill to give the vote to working men. Meetings were organised all over the North and Midlands. Some speakers called for a People's Parliament and a national strike. There were even riots in Hyde Park. Railings were torn down and crowds clashed with police. But these were exceptions. Mostly the campaign was peaceful.

In 1867, Parliament finally did what had been unthinkable twenty years earlier. They gave most working men in towns the right to vote. Overnight the number of voters almost doubled to 2 million.

> There are always a few EXTREMISTS who spoil things, aren't there? If we don't give them the vote now the extremists may get the upper hand and we'll be threatened by revolution again.

AN ELECTION IN 1867

Were the Chartists right about the vote?

1867 REFORM ACT
Working men get the vote!

and up!

and up

builds up

Pressure from below
(ordinary people)

1832
THE 'GREAT'
REFORM
ACT   Middle-class men got the vote. No reforms for ordinary people

1848 PETITION

1848 DEMONSTRATION

1842 RIOTS IN HALIFAX

1842 PETITION

1839 PETITION

1839 RIOTS IN BIRMINGHAM AND NEWPORT

1870
EDUCATION ACT
Councils to build schools all over Britain

1871
BANK HOLIDAYS ACT
By law, everyone is given holidays from work

1872
SECRET BALLOT
Voting now in secret. This cuts out bribes

1875
PUBLIC HEALTH ACT
All towns must provide clean water and dispose of sewage and waste

1891
EDUCATION ACT
No one has to pay to go to school

So all that effort by my father and his father was worthwhile. I got the vote and all these reforms followed. Voting **is** power.

It's all right for you. I still can't vote.

DISCUSS

O'Connor believed that once working men had the right to vote, the other problems would be solved. Was he right? The demand for reform built up, like rumbling lava in a volcano. The volcano finally exploded in 1867 when working men were given the vote. After that, reforms showered down on the people.

1 Why do you think governments passed all of these reforms **after 1867**?
2 Do you think that violent methods or peaceful methods did more to win the vote for men?

◆ Your advertising campaign: the posters

Your Campaign ▼ POSTER 1

Your campaign needs posters. They could be for a poster site, a bus shelter or a train station.

Poster 1

You could use one of the improvements in the 1870s due to voting. Use the ideas on this page to help you. Your teacher may also give you a checklist to work through. Remember to consider the points opposite.

Successful posters are very carefully put together. Pictures and captions are selected to get their message across. They are the ones we can all remember.

Look at this poster and in pairs discuss your answers to the questions around the poster.

What audience is the poster aimed at?

What gives the poster impact?

Why are contrasting colours used for the two rooms?

What images in the poster make the audience feel happy and well off?

What fears does the poster create in the audience if they don't vote?

If your great-grandparents had not fought for the right to vote, you might have been living here! **VOTING MATTERS!**

Why are the key words 'great-grandparents' and 'fought' in the caption?

Why are the words 'living here' on the right-hand half of the poster?

How to make a poster

Think about:

◆ **Location** Where will the poster go? At a bus stop, where people may wait for ten minutes and have time to read it, or on a billboard by the side of a busy road, where people go past quickly?

◆ **Audience** What age range is your poster targeted at? Young people, older people, or those in their 20s and 30s? Does it target men or women, or both equally?

◆ **Slogans** A poster needs a short, snappy slogan. What slogan will you use? (See below.)

◆ **Colour** There should be good use of a few contrasting colours – too many colours take your eye away from the point of the poster.

◆ **Imagery** Images must be eye-catching and simple. If they are complicated people will not bother trying to understand them.

Snappy, Short, Snazzy Slogans!

This heading uses alliteration. The letter 'S' is repeated to give impact to the heading. Often adverts use alliteration in slogans to get you to remember the product they are advertising. The poster opposite could have 'People Power' as the slogan to suggest that men who could vote after 1867 had the power to force governments to take action such as cleaning up the towns.

Alternatively, as we have called your campaign 'Voting Matters', you could use that as your slogan.

◆ Your advertising campaign: the leaflet

"You have seen the struggle working men and women had to get the vote. You have seen the sort of conditions we lived in and the hard, dangerous jobs we did. I hope you have understood our story, the methods we used in our campaigns and the problems we faced from people with power. You now have a very good idea why we fought so desperately and why some people even died for the vote. After studying this section you will be able to explain to your friends, parents and teachers why the vote was important to us. I am sure you agree that it is a story that everyone should hear!"

Your leaflet will explain why people today have a duty to use their vote that thousands fought for and some died for.

The leaflet will have four pages:

Page 1: The front cover will have a picture of your chosen hero or heroine and a catchy slogan (see pages 33 and 64–65).

Page 2: 'They died for you!' This will explain some of the reasons why people were willing to die for the vote in the 1830s and 1840s (see page 35 opposite).

Page 3: 'Votes for Women!' will deal with the reasons why women fought and died in the early 1900s (see page 41).

Page 4: 'Use your vote!' will persuade people to vote today (see page 61).

ACTIVITY

Page 2: They died for you!

1 Start with two or three sentences to grip the reader stating briefly and factually the actions men and women took in order to have the vote. You need to make this persuasive. Write so that the reader will be sympathetic towards people from this time and will know why the vote was important. An example might be:

Men and women all over Britain died so that we can have freedom today.

2 Remember that as well as the people who died, there were a lot of Chartists and strikers sent to jail or to Australia. So add a sentence or two to include these actions. Be bold and dramatic at the start of your paragraph.

3 Next, write a few sentences to explain the reasons why voting was so important to people in the 1830s and 1840s. Think about poor housing, long hours at work, disease and the dreaded workhouse. Pages 10–13 and 20–23 might be useful.

Tips for your writing!

You are dealing with several topics and need different ways to start sentences. Use phrases such as:

Similarly, work was . . .
Equally, housing for most people was . . .
In the same way . . .

You may want to point out one social problem as the most important by saying:

Above all . . .
More important was . . .
In particular . . .

Finish by explaining who could and could not vote in the 1830s. To make your point stronger, use evidence from the Chartists about why they were willing to die or go to prison for this right. Link the second and third sections with starters such as:

What is more . . .
More importantly . . .

End this first page with a firm voice using words such as:

Obviously . . .
Clearly . . .
Surely . . .

Before you start, look through the following list of techniques that you can use when you need to write persuasively.

- Sound assertive or convincing, to show you are sure of your view and in no doubt about the point you are making.
- Use facts to support your argument or explanation, e.g. ages of child workers, deaths from cholera or the low numbers of people allowed to vote.
- Use emotive language to arouse strong feelings in the reader, e.g. shock, anger, sadness, sympathy.
- Use repetition of a few words or phrases to emphasise points.
- Use slogans.
- Use headings, side headings and underlining to make points.
- Use exclamation marks for emphasis.
- Make a long list of facts clearer by using bullet points.
- Ask rhetorical questions. They don't expect an answer but are used for effect, for example 'The government didn't care, did it?'

Morpeth, Northumberland, 15 June 1913. The route to the graveyard ran down a quiet country road. The procession filed slowly through the dense crowds of people. Masses of men and women had been streaming into Morpeth since an early hour of the morning. They waited with bared and bowed heads to see her coffin pass. Many were in tears.

They had come to the funeral of Emily Wilding Davison, suffragette. Eleven days earlier, she had run in front of the King's horse during the Derby horse race, the most famous race in the year. She had been trying to stop the King's horse, to draw attention to the suffragettes' campaign for 'Votes for Women'. Bowled over by the horse, she suffered severe head injuries and died four days later. Emily Davison had died for the vote. See pages 52–53 for the full story.

People were so shocked by Emily Davison's death that this was her second funeral service. The previous day London had come to a halt as her coffin was carried through the streets to a church service. Hundreds of thousands of Londoners watched as column after column of suffragettes walked behind the coffin, their banners declaring 'Fight on and God will give the victory'.

ACTIVITY

In Section 2 you will investigate how women campaigned to win the vote in the early 1900s. One important part of studying history is learning to ask questions to guide and structure your investigation. What questions do you want to ask about the suffragettes' campaign?

How could you use the information on this page to help you with the advertising campaign? Note down a few ideas that might be useful for your TV advert, posters or leaflet.

Your Campaign
▼
VOTING MATTERS!

WHY DID WOMEN DIE FOR THE VOTE?

◆ What was the Victorians' idea of the 'Ideal Woman'?

Angelic
A wife provided a safe and loving home for her children and husband. The Victorians called the wife 'the angel in the house'.

Obedient
A wife obeyed her husband in everything. A famous Victorian writer said 'The true destiny of a woman . . . is to wed a man she can love.'

A possession
When a woman married, her money, her possessions and even the woman herself legally became her husband's property.

Pale and delicate
A wife was expected to look slim and delicate. Pale skin was the sign of a well-bred young woman. Tanned skin was a sign of a woman working.

Silent
A woman was not expected to attend meetings or speak about politics. That was because women were seen by many as less intelligent than men. The scientist T. H. Huxley said, 'In every way whether physical or mental, the average woman is inferior to the average man.'

Separate
The Victorians spoke about men and women having 'separate spheres'. A man's sphere was outside the home, working and earning enough to look after his family. A woman's sphere was inside the home, creating a welcoming home for her husband. Women were not expected to work outside the house.

SOURCE I George Hick's painting *Woman's Mission: Companion of Manhood*, 1863, which illustrates what middle-class Victorians thought the ideal wife should be like.

ACTIVITY A

1 What does the title of the painting tell us about how the artist saw the role of women in the nineteenth century?
2 Do you think that all women could live like this 'ideal'? Give reasons for your answer.
3 Imagine you are the editor of a magazine for middle-class married women in the nineteenth century. What would you include on your contents page for the Christmas 1864 issue to help women live up to this ideal?
4 Compare your ideas for a nineteenth-century magazine with the contents pages of magazines aimed at married women today. What has stayed the same? What is different?

In 1900 women could not vote. Most men did not believe that women should have the right to vote. Here are some of their arguments.

WHY WOMEN SHOULD NOT BE ALLOWED TO VOTE

ACTIVITY B

1 Put yourself into the shoes of a woman who wanted the vote. Write down what you would say in reply to the arguments below. You can get a sheet from your teacher to help you.

2 Construct a timeline to show the main events in the late 1800s and early 1900s as women fought for the right to vote. Your teacher can give you a sheet with some dates to start you off. You can add to the timeline as you work through Section 2.

1 Women don't need to vote. Men look after women's interests. We've made laws limiting the hours women work in factories and now we let women go to university. Men can be trusted to run the country.

2 Women shouldn't go out to work because they take jobs from men. This doesn't do anyone any good because women earn less than men so the families have less money.

3 The majority of women don't want the vote. It's just a noisy few that are demanding women's rights. My husband looks after me perfectly well. I don't know what he earns but I get a good allowance for clothes.

4 Man was created by God to rule over woman. This is God's eternal law which we have no right to alter.

5 Women are irrational, hysterical and not capable of making important decisions therefore they should not have the vote.

If a woman has the vote, she will devote less time to her family. The house will be untidy, the children in rags and there will be no dinner on the table.

Women are weaker than men in their physical strength. Women do not fight in wars so they do not have the right to vote.

◆ Why did women need the vote?

Emmeline Pankhurst campaigned for women to have the vote. She started the Women's Social and Political Union in 1903. Its members were called the SUFFRAGETTES. Suffrage means the right to vote. She used actions as well as words to draw attention to the cause of 'Votes for Women'.

"Women need the vote to achieve equal rights. We want better living and working conditions. Having the vote brings improvements. In 1867 working men won the vote so the government built schools, trade unions were made legal and hours of work were cut. But because women don't have the vote, Parliament ignores us. Just look at the things we women have to put up with."

Education

After 1870 government schools were built for boys and girls under ten years old. It cost a few pence a week to send a child to school. All children were taught to read and write but in 1878 a new law said that all girls must be taught 'domestic economy'. This meant lessons in washing, ironing, cooking, cleaning and making beds. Girls had more absence from school than boys because they were expected to do housework and look after younger children.

SOURCE 3 A woman graduate in 1893.

Sons of well-off families went to fee-paying schools. By the 1880s middle-class girls were also going to schools and being taught science and mathematics. These women became teachers and secretaries but they had to resign when they got married. It was thought wrong for married women to work outside the home. Some girls went to university if their parents supported them. A few became doctors and architects but they were paid a lot less than men doing the same job. Women were not allowed to be lawyers or work in banks.

SOURCE 2 A domestic economy lesson for girls only c.1890.

Women's work

Not all women could be 'the angel in the house'. Working-class women had to work because their families depended on them earning money. On average, women earned half the wages of men.

Most girls left school at twelve years old and many went to work as servants. One woman in eight was a servant in 1871. Most servants were young, unmarried and poorly paid. The hours were long, from 5 o'clock in the morning until 11 o'clock at night, and many had only one afternoon off a month.

There had been some improvements. Women at a match factory in London went on strike in 1889, because the pay was very poor and the dust gave them cancer. They won more money and better conditions. This was a good example of women sticking together and fighting for their rights. It inspired others to do the same!

SOURCE 4 Many women worked in cotton mills.

ACTIVITY A

Use the evidence on pages 38–41 to make three lists:

a) things women were allowed to do
b) things women were not allowed to do
c) things women were expected to do.

◆ *Your advertising campaign: the leaflet*

ACTIVITY B

Page 3: Votes for Women!

You will be using the information in Section 2 to write page 3 of your leaflet, Votes for Women'. Write in the same style as you did for page 2 of your leaflet (see page 35). Start paragraph 1 now and add the rest as you work through Units 2.2 and 2.3.

Paragraph 1: a short gripping introduction. Write a few sentences explaining why women needed the vote. Use pages 38–41 to help you. **Paragraph 2:** show how women campaigned for the vote, the different methods they used, including dying for the cause. Use pages 42–53 to help you. **Paragraph 3:** short concluding sentence to remind readers of the message, 'women died for the vote!' Remember to use the persuasive writing tips from page 35. Your teacher may give you a sheet to remind you of the layout for your page.

Your Campaign ▼ THE LEAFLET

◆ Who started the suffragettes . . .

From the 1850s suffrage societies campaigned for women to be able to vote. They joined together as a national organisation called the National Union of Women's Suffrage Societies (NUWSS). They were called SUFFRAGISTS. They used letters to newspapers and MPs, leaflets, marches to London to see the Prime Minister, and petitions to persuade MPs to support them. They had lots of MPs on their side but despite these tactics women still did not have the vote.

In October 1903, Emmeline Pankhurst set up a new society, the Women's Social and Political Union (WSPU). They decided to limit their membership exclusively to women. 'Deeds not Words' was to be their motto. They became known as the suffragettes.

In 1906 the suffragettes moved their headquarters from Manchester to London. They hoped this would give them a better chance to influence Parliament, the law courts and the main newspapers, which were all in London.

Who were the Pankhursts?

Emmeline Pankhurst

"I was born in 1858 in Manchester into a well-off family. When I was 21 I married a lawyer, Richard Pankhurst. We have five children. Christabel was my first daughter."

Christabel Pankhurst

"I was one of the few women to train as a lawyer in the 1890s but I am not allowed to work as a lawyer. I believe the suffragettes should be more militant. We need actions. Talking has got us nowhere."

Sylvia Pankhurst

"I trained as an artist. I am a member of the new Labour Party. My mother disapproves of me spending so much time with poor working women, but we should be fighting to make better laws for all women as well as for the vote."

◆ *. . . and who joined them?*

Thousands of women, rich and poor, joined the suffragettes.
Here is a selection.

SOURCE 1 Annie Kenney (1879–1953). A mill-worker from Lancashire, she was the only working-class woman to become a suffragette leader. Since she was ten, Annie had worked half of each day in a mill and spent half a day at school. She became famous in 1905 when, together with Christabel Pankhurst, she was arrested and imprisoned for shouting out at a political meeting. This was the first militant action of the suffragettes. Annie was imprisoned four times.

SOURCE 2 Mary Gawthorpe (1881–1960). Born into a poor family in Leeds, she became a teacher and worked hard for poor needy children as well as for the suffragettes. She went to prison four times. In 1912 she went on hunger strike in protest at how the suffragettes were being treated. She was released early because of her poor health.

SOURCE 3 Indian suffragettes at the Women's Coronation Procession in 1911. This procession was held a week before the coronation of King George V to win publicity for 'Votes for Women'.

ACTIVITY

1 Make a list of words that you think describe the suffragettes on these two pages.
2 A number of different methods of campaigning that the suffragettes used are mentioned on these two pages. Over pages 44–53 you will find out many more. As you go, compile a table like this:

Suffragettes' actions	Government methods to stop suffragettes

◆ *How did the suffragettes get publicity?*

Suffragette activity can be summed up in one word – **publicity**. Most MPs were actually in favour of votes for women, but it was an issue they could easily ignore. So the Pankhursts wanted to make votes for women an issue they could not ignore. This meant publicity, publicity, publicity. They wanted their campaign to be on the front page of the newspapers every day if possible. Here are just a few of the things they did.

SOURCE 4 **Chaining to railings** Suffragettes chained themselves to railings so that they had more time to protest before police took them away.

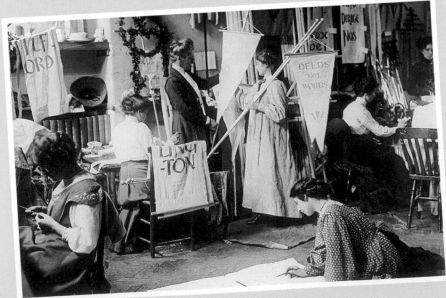

SOURCE 5 **Banners** The suffragettes insisted banners should be made skilfully and with good materials. Their rules were: 'Never use anything that is ugly', 'If it is not exactly right it won't do at all', 'Do not use the wrong colour'.

SOURCE 6

Newspapers The suffragettes published their own weekly newspaper *Votes for Women*. It was sold in shops all over Britain and on the street by suffragette members. Women had to stand in the street to sell their newspaper because they could be arrested for obstruction if they stood on the pavement. The newspaper had pictures and articles about suffragette processions and meetings, fund-raising reports and letters. Prizes of bicycles painted in the suffragette colours were given to the women who sold the most copies.

SOURCE 7 **Processions** In 1908, 300,000 suffragettes joined a march to Hyde Park. The marchers wore white, green and purple as a uniform. Six brass and silver bands played suffragette songs.

SOURCE 9 **Photo opportunities** Christabel Pankhurst buying heather to welcome the 'Scotch lassie' Mary Phillips on her release from prison in 1908. She was the longest-serving suffragette prisoner.

SOURCE 8 **Chalking** Emma Sproson and a friend chalking a suffragette message in the suffragette colours of purple, white and green in 1907.

ACTIVITY

1 Add these methods to your table from page 43.
2 Which of the activities in Sources 4–9 do you think would:
   a) get more members
   b) make the suffragettes feel united
   c) spread the suffragette message?

Photographs as evidence
Photographs are an important source of evidence for historians but should we believe what they are showing us? Work in pairs or groups of three.

3 a) Choose one photograph on pages 42–45. Why do you think the suffragettes wanted it taken?
   b) Suffragette supporters took these photographs. Does this affect their value to historians?
4 What do you think are
   a) the advantages and
   b) the disadvantages of photographs as evidence for historians?

SOURCE 11
Suffragette badge.

◆ Purple, white and green

The suffragettes needed a lot of money to pay full-time workers, print leaflets, hire meeting halls and spread their PROPAGANDA. Suffragette shops made money selling a range of goods and the profits went to the 'war-chest'. These goods also helped publicise their campaign.

Source 10 shows a typical shop. Other shops sold suffragette cigarettes, soap, chocolate, playing cards, games and stationery. Most items were in the suffragette colours of purple, white and green. These were chosen deliberately. Purple was for dignity, white represented purity and green was the sign of living things – hope for the future. The colours were very important to identify with the suffragettes, to show that you were a supporter!

SOURCE 12 The suffragette emblem was designed by Sylvia Pankhurst. The tea set was made in Staffordshire where the best china was made.

SOURCE 10 Suffragette goods on sale in The Women's Press shop including tea, postcard albums and a suffragette kite.

SOURCE 13 A silk scarf. It could be used in several ways: as a scarf, round the shoulders, or to wrap around your hat if out in one of the new open-topped cars.

SOURCE 15 This poster was also available as a postcard.

SOURCE 14 A suffragette Christmas card.

ACTIVITY B

1 Draw up a chart like the one below and complete it showing how the suffragettes used their merchandise to achieve each aim.

Aim	Suffragette merchandise
A clear identity for the organisation	
Attract a range of people	
Use the latest technology	
Present the faces of your stars	

2 If you had gone to a suffragette shop and had come out with
 a) a scarf
 b) a badge and
 c) a poster
 on what occasions might you use them and why?

3 Which of these statements do the photographs on pages 44–47 support?
 a) The suffragette movement was well-organised.
 b) The suffragettes had lots of support.
 c) Suffragette activities were peaceful.
 d) Suffragette supporters were rich.
 Explain your answer using evidence from the sources.

◆ How did the campaign become more violent after 1910?

November 1910 was a turning point in the campaign. The Prime Minister promised to change the law so that women had the right to vote. It looked as if victory was in their grasp. Then he called an election so the plan was abandoned. The suffragettes were furious and frustrated.

On 18 November 1910, 300 women went to Parliament to protest. They were beaten up by police who had been ordered by the government to frighten and humiliate the women so they would stop protests. Police kicked the women, twisted their breasts, punched their noses and thrust knees between their legs. One woman, Ellen Pitfield, died from her injuries.

From 1910 the suffragette campaign became more MILITANT. In the past a few suffragettes had attacked property or smashed windows. Now that became common. In the past, one or two suffragette leaders had risked prison. Now it became hundreds.

Emmeline Pankhurst called the suffragettes an 'army'. The women were referred to as 'warriors'. Money raised went to the 'war-chest'. Over the next four years:

- ◆ Street lamps were broken.
- ◆ Keyholes were stopped up with lead pellets.
- ◆ House numbers were painted out.
- ◆ Golf greens were scraped and burnt with acid.
- ◆ Telegraph and telephone wires were severed with long-handled clippers.
- ◆ Thirteen pictures were hacked in the Manchester Art Gallery.
- ◆ Houses were set on fire.
- ◆ Bombs were placed near the Bank of England in London, in Doncaster and in Dublin.
- ◆ An axe was thrown at the Prime Minister.

SOURCE 16 Suffragettes with a smashed window in 1912.

From 1911 the suffragettes set out on massive window-smashing raids. Many of the shops in the West End of London were attacked. On 1 March 1912 Emmeline Pankhurst and others smashed windows in 10 Downing Street, the home of the Prime Minister, and on the same day 150 shops were attacked. One elderly woman gave this as her reason for becoming more violent: 'I've read everything; a great deal has been written, and a great deal has been said and it's no good. Something has got to be done! I just want to go out into the street and smash, and smash, and smash – everything.'

SOURCE 17 **Arson** Several racecourse stands were set on fire. The suffragettes made sure there were no people or animals in these properties. Police often found suffragette leaflets and posters at the scene but rarely managed to arrest a suffragette. Many acts of arson took place in 1913 in protest about Emmeline Pankhurst being arrested.

SOURCE 19 **Hunger strikes** Because of the increased violence there were many suffragettes in prison. To win sympathy, suffragette prisoners began a mass hunger strike in June 1912.

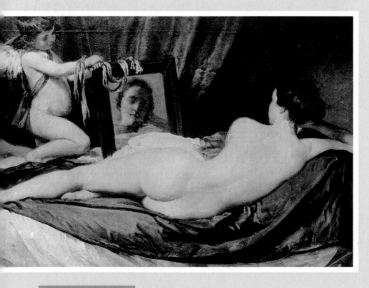

SOURCE 18 **Picture slashing** Mary Richardson felt that men valued objects more than they valued giving women the vote. 'A painting came to mind. Yes, yes, the *Venus* in the National Gallery. As the day approached I grew nervous. The hours of hesitation were brought unexpectedly to an end by an announcement in the evening newspaper. "Mrs. Pankhurst taken from a meeting in Glasgow." I went out to spend my last shillings on an axe.' Mary Richardson slashed the painting seven times.

ACTIVITY

1 Using Sources 16–19 add these actions to the chart that you started on page 43.

2 Does the evidence on these two pages suggest that:
   a) the suffragettes thought carefully about violent actions before taking them, or
   b) the suffragettes acted on impulse?
   Support your answer with evidence from the sources.

3 Do you agree with the statement 'The only reason the suffragettes became more violent was to get more publicity'? Use evidence from these pages to help you write your answer.

4 For each of the actions in Sources 16–19 suggest what would be the most sensible way for the government to deal with the protesters.

5 Captions affect how we interpret or think about photographs. Choose one of the photographs on this page and write two captions to go with it – one written by a suffragette, the other by a member of the government opposed to the suffragettes.

49

◆ *How did opponents react to the suffragettes' campaign?*

B

In line with the government's wishes the management inform the public they will allow no further suffragette meetings in this hall.

TOWN HALL

C

Women are only allowed in if accompanied by a responsible man.

ART GALLERY

A

Over 150 women made statements accusing the police of brutality on Black Friday and they were supported by independent witnesses. One statement said: 'For hours I was beaten about the body, thrown backwards and forwards from one policeman to another. I was pushed into a side street where I was beaten up and down my spine while he said "I will teach you not to come back any more. I will punish you, you . . ." I was thrown with my jaw against a lamp-post so my front teeth were loosened.'

D I sentence you to eighteen months' imprisonment for this outrageous offence.

E These women thrive on publicity. Please make sure your newspaper reports are not sympathetic to these women.

Votes for Women

SOURCE 20

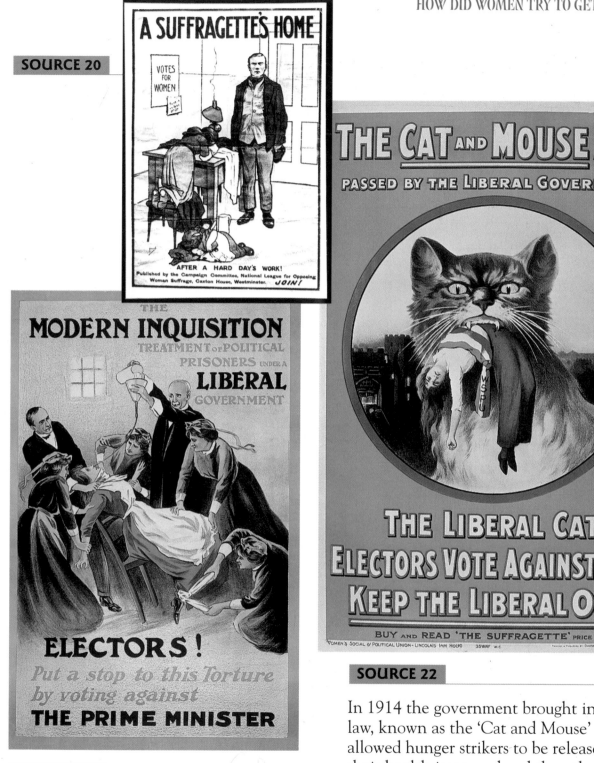

A SUFFRAGETTE'S HOME

VOTES FOR WOMEN

AFTER A HARD DAY'S WORK!

Published by the Campaign Committee, National League for Opposing Woman Suffrage, Caxton House, Westminster. JOIN!

THE MODERN INQUISITION

TREATMENT OF POLITICAL PRISONERS UNDER A LIBERAL GOVERNMENT

ELECTORS!

Put a stop to this Torture by voting against

THE PRIME MINISTER

THE CAT AND MOUSE ACT

PASSED BY THE LIBERAL GOVERNMENT

WSPU

THE LIBERAL CAT ELECTORS VOTE AGAINST HIM! KEEP THE LIBERAL OUT!

BUY AND READ 'THE SUFFRAGETTE' PRICE 1P.

WOMEN'S SOCIAL & POLITICAL UNION – LINCOLNS INN HOUSE   35 WAY W.C.

SOURCE 21

This poster shows a hunger striker being forcibly fed. The woman was held down and a tube was pushed up her nose. A milky liquid was poured into a funnel connected to the rubber tube. This was extremely painful. The government ordered force-feeding to stop hunger strikers dying as this would cause a lot of bad publicity.

SOURCE 22

In 1914 the government brought in a new law, known as the 'Cat and Mouse' Act. This allowed hunger strikers to be released until their health improved and then they would be re-arrested to complete their sentences.

ACTIVITY B

Look at Sources 20, 21 and 22. For each source explain:
a) who you think produced the poster
b) who they were trying to influence
c) how they got their message across.
What can a historian learn from these sources?

◆ *Emily Davison – martyr!*

Emily Davison was a teacher. She gave up her career to campaign full time for the suffragettes. She believed the suffragettes were right to be militant. She was put in prison nine times for stone throwing, window smashing and setting fire to post boxes. While in prison she went on hunger strike.

Then in 1913 she planned her most ambitious protest yet – a grand gesture, at the world-famous Derby horse race at Epsom. In full view of the royal family, and of journalists from around the world she would . . .

. . . she would **what**? Well, that is for you to work out.

SOURCE 23 From the front page of *Lloyd's Weekly News*, 8 June 1913.

SOURCE 24 Further evidence to consider.

a) *The police found the following items on her person:*

- ◆ *a return ticket from Epsom to London*
- ◆ *a ticket to a suffragette event in London later that day*
- ◆ *a race card which she had marked up showing which horses she expected to win*
- ◆ *two enormous suffragette banners pinned to the inside of her jacket.*

b) *Pictures of the event show that she ran onto the course and stood sideways waiting for the king's horse to come by.*

c) *In previous weeks Emily Davison had been seen stopping horses on the common in her home town of Morpeth and pinning suffragette pennants to them.*

ACTIVITY

You are part of the police team investigating this incident. Using Sources 23 and 24, see if you can work out:
a) what actually happened on 4 June
b) what Emily Davison meant to happen.
You can also refer to pages 36–37.

Emily Davison's skull was fractured by the horse's hooves. For three days she lay unconscious in a hospital bed. The suffragette leaders were stunned. Emily Davison had not talked about her plans to anyone. They did not know what to make of these events.

On 8 June, Emily Davison died. Now she had become a martyr. A martyr is someone who dies for a cause they believe in. The suffragette publicity machine went into action. They staged two massive funerals: one in London and one at Emily Davison's home town in Morpeth (see page 36). They ran a special edition of their newspaper (Source 26).

Even the attitude of the newspapers changed. Just days earlier *The Times* newspaper had been angry and scornful of Emily Davison. Now the *Sunday Times* called her 'the most unassuming and gentlest of creatures, though she possessed a spirit capable of heroic deed and sacrifice'.

SOURCE 26   Extract from *The Suffragette*, 13 June 1913.

Millions of people had their attention riveted on the race. Miss Davison seized the opportunity, and with incredible courage made a protest which has fired the imagination and touched the hearts of people. Her act has proved more eloquent than all the words of all the speeches could be . . . She has taught the world that there are women who care so passionately for the vote and all it means that they are willing to die for it.

D I S C U S S

1 Compare Sources 25 and 27. How do they differ in their interpretation of the death of Emily Davison?
2 If you were working for *The Suffragette* newspaper which of the two pictures would you choose to go with Source 26? Give your reasons.
3 Do you think Emily Davison was incredibly brave or incredibly foolish? Give your reasons.
4 How might this event be useful in your publicity campaign?

SOURCE 25

SOURCE 27

SOURCE 1

◆ What did the suffragettes do during the war?

Women responded in different ways to the announcement that Britain was at war with Germany. Many decided to join in the war effort and volunteered for a variety of jobs but others decided that all fighting was wrong and would not do any kind of war work (people who believed this were known as pacifists).

Many followers of Emmeline and Christabel Pankhurst decided to stop campaigning for the vote and became very enthusiastic volunteers for a whole range of work to help fight the war on the 'Home Front'. A government minister asked Emmeline Pankhurst to organise a recruitment march that would encourage women to offer to work. This was very successful.

SOURCE 2

SOURCE 3

SOURCE 4

SOURCE 5

ACTIVITY B

You have looked at a large number of photographs in this section.

1 What kinds of evidence do photographs provide for historians?

2 What can photographs NOT tell us about the suffragette movement?

3 Compare the photographs in this section with the photograph of the Chartist meeting on pages 26–27.
   a) How are the photographs different?
   b) Can you work out how photography had changed between 1848 and 1900?

4 Why were photographs valuable to
   a) the suffragettes and
   b) their opponents?

◆ Why did women get the vote?

Women had helped to win the war and some of them were allowed to vote for the first time in 1918 when 6 million women aged over 30 voted in the general election. Women had been campaigning for this day since the 1860s. However, there was not one simple reason why women had won the vote.

Why did women get the vote? The work done by women in the war was definitely one reason. Women had taken an active part in war work both at home and overseas. The poem on page 57 tells you about some of the 'men's' jobs carried out by women in the war.

AN ELECTION IN 1918

SOURCE 6 'War Girls' by Jessie Pope.

There's the girl who clips your ticket for the train,
And the girl who speeds the lift from floor to floor.
There's the girl who does a milk-round in the rain,
And the girl who calls for orders at your door.
Strong, sensible and fit,
They're out to show their grit,
And tackle jobs with energy and knack.
No longer caged up and penned up,
They're going to keep their end up
Till the khaki soldier boys come marching back.

So the vote was partly a reward for working in the war. The government had already started to think about giving women the vote in 1915 when the peaceful NUWSS wrote thousands of letters to MPs. Their leader, Millicent Fawcett, had decided it would not be right to hold demonstrations during wartime. Many MPs were impressed by their lack of violence and began to support votes for women. Herbert Asquith was the most important of those MPs because he was Prime Minister for the first two years of the war.

Women cannot fight but they fill our munition factories. They are doing work which the fighting men had to perform before and this makes a special appeal to me. Since the war began we have had no recurrence of that detestable campaign and no one can say we are giving in to violence.

There was a whole range of other reasons why women won the vote:

◆ David Lloyd George, who replaced Herbert Asquith as Prime Minister in 1916, was a supporter of women voting but not the use of violence.
◆ The Labour Party, which had always supported women voting, had MPs in the wartime government.
◆ Men who had organised anti-suffrage groups were away in the war and could not influence what was happening at home.
◆ *The Times* newspaper supported 'Votes for Women' when it could see women working hard in the war.

The WSPU (the suffragettes), with our pre-war campaign for the vote, followed by our patriotic stand and national service, has won the greatest victory on record.

ACTIVITY

1 Make a list of the reasons given for why women got the vote in 1918.
2 Do you agree with Emmeline Pankhurst that the suffragettes' action won women the right to vote? Explain your answer using evidence from what you have learned. Your teacher will give you a sheet to help you write a well-thought-out answer.

You are probably wondering why only women over 30 were given the vote in 1918. There were two reasons. Firstly, the government didn't want there to be more women voting than men. If all women over 21 had been given the vote then 52 per cent of voters would have been women. Secondly, some men still believed that women, especially when they were young, were not capable of understanding serious matters like politics. The government feared that MPs would stop women having the vote at the same age as men. Women over 21 were eventually given the vote in 1928.

CONCLUSIONS

3.1 DID VOTING MAKE A DIFFERENCE?

The struggle for the vote was long and hard. But what would have happened if everyone had been like the parents on pages 2–3 who could not be bothered to go to meetings?

In 1800 only men who owned land could vote and be MPs so only one man in ten had the vote. The government did not do anything about the lives of ordinary people.

But once ordinary people were allowed to vote, governments started to take notice of them. After all, the voters had the power to get rid of a government that did not care about them.

Today all men and women over the age of 18 can vote in a SECRET BALLOT for MPs, for their local councillors and for Members of the European Parliament. Elections for Parliament must take place every five years. If only rich men could still vote we would not have had these changes in the last 130 years:

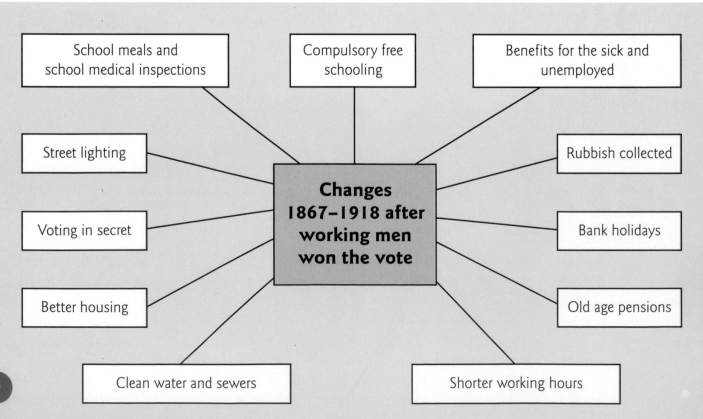

School meals and school medical inspections

Compulsory free schooling

Benefits for the sick and unemployed

Street lighting

Rubbish collected

Voting in secret

Changes 1867–1918 after working men won the vote

Bank holidays

Better housing

Old age pensions

Clean water and sewers

Shorter working hours

◆ Your advertising campaign: the posters

Adverts often work because they promise us success or better lives if we buy a particular product. For example, they try to persuade us that we might be more attractive, happier or have more friends if we use a particular fragrance, buy a certain type of drink or wear a certain make of clothes.

Your Campaign ▼ POSTER 2

Poster 2

The second poster for the campaign must show one of the improvements to women's lives because they could vote in elections. The idea is to persuade women to vote by showing them that voting got changes in the past and now they too have power by using their vote.

Design a poster showing one thing that changed for women because they could vote. Make it simple, eye catching and bright. Think carefully where it will be used, the target age group and remember to use a few well-chosen words for your slogan. Look back to pages 32–33 for some tips on planning your poster.

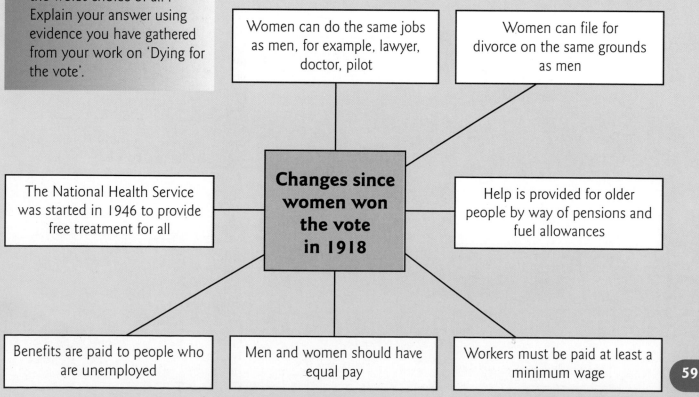

Women can do the same jobs as men, for example, lawyer, doctor, pilot

Women can file for divorce on the same grounds as men

Changes since women won the vote in 1918

The National Health Service was started in 1946 to provide free treatment for all

Help is provided for older people by way of pensions and fuel allowances

Benefits are paid to people who are unemployed

Men and women should have equal pay

Workers must be paid at least a minimum wage

Voting is a powerful way of making your voice heard. In the past people like the Chartists and suffragettes didn't have the vote. They held demonstrations, organised petitions, were sentenced to prison, force-fed, transported to Australia and even died to get the vote.

One vote on its own may not seem much but millions of votes mean power and that means governments have to listen to what people want. In some countries people have only recently got the vote. In others people are still willing to die to get it – that's how important the vote is.

Until 1994, black people in South Africa did not have the right to vote. The governments had always been white and laws kept black and white people apart. Black people were treated as second class. These laws were called the apartheid laws. After years of demonstrations, imprisonments and pressure from other countries, black people were finally allowed to vote. Many people walked for miles to vote and, when they got to the polling station, waited for hours to use their vote. Today South Africa has a black majority in government that is gradually improving the houses, schools and health of the majority of the population.

ACTIVITY

1 a) Why are some people's attitudes to the vote different today in South Africa and Britain?
   b) Why are attitudes to the vote in Britain today different from in the 1840s?
2 In Australia anyone who does not vote has to pay a fine. Is this a good idea?

SOURCE 1 Black South African voters queuing in the 1994 elections.

◆ *Your advertising campaign: the final touches*

You now need to complete your advertising campaign to persuade people that voting is important. You need to produce a final poster, the last page of your leaflet and a TV advert.

Your Campaign ▼ **POSTER 3**

Your Campaign ▼ **THE LEAFLET**

Daddy, what did __YOU__ do in the Great War?

Poster 3
In the First World War the government put out posters like this to shock people and to make them feel guilty if they did not play their part.

Use the fact that Chartists and suffragettes died to get the vote. Design a poster for the campaign that will shock people into voting.

- ◆ Make them feel guilty if they do not vote.
- ◆ Persuade the audience that voting is a duty, that they owe it to those who sacrificed their lives in the past.

You will need to look back at Section 1 for how Chartists were treated, especially pages 24–25, and at Section 2 for the suffragettes, especially pages 36–37 and 50–51.

Page 4: Use your vote!
Design and write your last page of the leaflet so that it will persuade people today that they should vote. One technique used in persuasive writing is to spell out a slogan or word down the page and to use each initial as a starter for the points you want to make, for example:

No compromise
Ordinary people fight
Win the vote!

The points have to be brief and punchy. Remember that this method of persuasion uses the idea of offering a change or a better life. These can be based on changes for individuals, such as higher wages, or for everyone, such as safer cities or a better health service.

◆ *Your advertising campaign: the TV advert*

This is the final challenge and the biggest challenge of your advertising campaign: a TV advertisement. You have been asked by the Director of the Schools History Project to make a 30-second advert to be shown in the week before the next general election. It will sum up in just 30 seconds the big lesson from history that **Voting Matters**!

Most TV adverts take weeks to make, involve dozens of people and cost hundreds of thousands of pounds. You have just yourself and your friends, no budget and maybe just one homework plus a lesson. But don't despair. It's your ideas that we are after, not a ritzy production. What we want is a storyboard like the one on page 63.

Making TV adverts: remember all these points . . .

Message
Must be a simple message. Just one clear idea for your viewers to remember. Just one good reason why they should vote. For example:

- ☐ The politicians will take no notice of you and will foul things up if you don't vote – play on people's fears.
- ☐ People in history died so that you can vote. Make people feel guilty if they stay at home.

Target audience
Decide who you are writing for:

- ☐ age range, e.g. new voters aged 18–23; your parents' age group; retired people aged 60 plus
- ☐ men or women or both
- ☐ working-class people or middle-class people.

What issues are your audience most bothered about?

Vision, sound and pace
Your TV advert must have:

- ☐ storyline: simple and gripping
- ☐ vision: a range of close-ups, medium and distance shots. Don't let the viewer get bored!
- ☐ sound: some shots will need lively music, some sad. If there is dialogue you will need to fade the music.
- ☐ pace: some shots need more time than others. Look at how we have done this in the storyboard.

You can do it . . . you can persuade those people to vote.

ACTIVITY

With a partner look at the storyboard.

1 How does frame 1 establish the age and target group for this advert?
2 How does background colour help make the viewer feel good?
3 According to the advert who will benefit from the couple going to vote?
4 Why do you think close-ups were used in frames such as 2 and 9?
5 Do you think this advert will succeed in making people vote?

Now it's your turn. Can you do better? Look at the checklist on the left then start working on your own ideas. Remember you can use as much or as little of the history from this book as you wish – but you must remember the big lesson from history: Voting Matters.

FRAME 1	Time 0–3 secs

Shot Bright sunny morning, blue skies, couple in summery clothes, school looks worn, shabby. Camera has school and couple in medium shot closing to close-up of children.

Sound Light happy music, not too loud.

FRAME 2	Time 4–5 secs

Shot Close-up of two young children with school in the background and the couple walking close by.

Sound One child says 'Thanks for doing it for us.'

FRAME 3	Time 6–9 secs

Shot Camera is long shot to show the park, couple in the distance.

Sound Music is lively to go with a feeling that life is good.

FRAME 4	Time 10–14 secs

Shot Close-up of the old man's face to show he is concerned and the young woman feels good about what he says.

Sound Old man saying to the young woman, 'We're so glad you did it. You did it for us.' Music fades for voices to be heard.

FRAME 5	Time 15–18 secs

Shot Medium, to pick out the nurses' uniforms as well as the young couple.

Sound Voices chattering with one saying, 'I hope everyone realises that they are doing it for the people in here.'

FRAME 6	Time 19–21 secs

Shot Close-up of the billboard and the message.

Sound A steady heartbeat to go with the hospital theme and to link frames 5 and 7.

FRAME 7	Time 22–25 secs

Shot Close-up shot showing nurses and couple talking. Shot is head to waist to include uniform and focus the viewers' attention on the theme of hospitals.

Sound One of the nurses says 'What you have done will help all of our patients. Thank you so much.'

FRAME 8	Time 26–28 secs

Shot Distance shot to get a feeling of a large crowd and the idea of an ordinary street – giving the idea that this could be anywhere in a typical town.

Sound Speech from a neighbour saying, 'Well done! We are all so pleased you did it.'

FRAME 9	Time 29–30 secs

Shot Close-up of couple on sofa showing them happy and pleased with themselves.

Sound Woman says, 'Voting is so worthwhile – it really does make a difference.' Music increases in volume to end the advert.

◆ Your advertising campaign: the leaflet

Who will be your hero or heroine?

There should now be space on the front cover of your leaflet. We intend you to fill it with a hero or heroine from the story of the fight for the vote.

Your Campaign ▼ THE LEAFLET COVER

ACTIVITY

Page 1: the cover star

1 Who will be your hero or heroine? On this page are some ideas to get you thinking but you do not have to choose one of these people. You can pick someone else entirely. When you have made your own decision hold a class vote to see who gets the most votes.

2 Discuss why people have different ideas about who they regard as heroes and heroines.

3 Write a suitable slogan for the front cover. Remember 'Snappy, Short, Snazzy Slogans!'

2 William Cuffay, the son of a West Indian slave. He joined the Chartists in 1836 and was transported to Australia in 1848 for 21 years for his part in leading the Chartists. His wife travelled out to join him and, after his release, he became a leader in the fight for workers' rights in Australia.

1 Feargus O'Connor, Chartist leader who died in 1855.

3 The Unknown Chartist. The men and women who gave their lives in wartime are commemorated at the grave of the unknown soldier. This Chartist represents all the people whose names we do not know who joined in the protests and meetings.

4 Emmeline, Christabel and Sylvia Pankhurst, suffragette leaders.

5 Emily Wilding Davison, suffragette martyr. Every 15 June, suffragettes travelled to Morpeth to remember her sacrifice. They carried on their 'Emily Davison Pilgrimage' until the late 1960s, 50 years later.

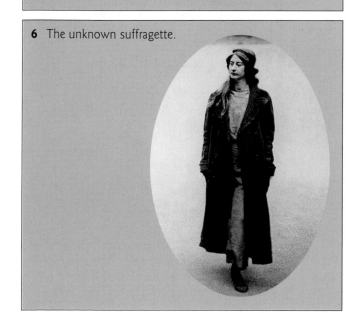

6 The unknown suffragette.

You could also think about including other people from history. This story did not begin with the Chartists. Before them, others were struggling to have more power over how the country was run. Can you remember anything about these two from your earlier study of history?

7 John Lilburne and the Levellers.
Remember us? We were the Levellers led by John Lilburne. We fought against the tyrant King Charles I in the Civil War in the 1640s. We wanted all men to have the vote even then. We failed. Lilburne and others went to prison and some of us were shot by Cromwell but our ideas lived on.

8 The people of the Peasants' Revolt of 1381.
We took part in the Peasants' Revolt in 1381. We were not fighting for the vote but for something even more basic – freedom. In our day, nearly half the people were VILLEINS and could not leave their village or marry without their lord's permission. They had to work on his land for at least two days a week without wages. We fought for freedom!

Of course you may have other ideas of your own from the rest of your course. Everyone has different ideas of what makes a hero or heroine.

An important piece of research carried out with two groups of history students aged 13–16 found some interesting ideas about what they believed they had got out of studying history. The two groups had been taught in very different ways and so it is not so surprising that they came up with different ideas about what the point of studying history is. Opposite are some of the answers given to the interviewer.

ACTIVITY

1 Look carefully at these interviews. On your own copy shade in the answers that you agree most with.
2 Compare your answers with a partner and discuss any differences of opinion you have. Suggest reasons why you either agree or disagree.
3 What examples from *Dying for the Vote* could these two people give to support their answers to the three questions? For example, the girl must write down some facts that have been learned and the boy must write down some reasons for people's actions.
4 Do you agree or disagree with these two comments? Explain your reasons.
   a) 'Knowing how to think is harder but usefuller than knowing lots of facts.'
   b) 'Ordinary people can only be important in history if we did something stupid or if I fell off a wall on top of somebody famous.'

Interviews

What do you think history is about?

You have to know the facts. The teacher tells you what happens or you read it in a book. It doesn't matter about why. Anyway you can't change it so why something happened is not important.

No, history is about why things happen. There are lots of reasons for events and actions. History helps us explain things.

Do you think events that you might be involved in or things you might experience would ever be recorded in history books?

Oh no, not in Castleford [in Yorkshire], maybe if I lived down south. We don't stand out enough, we don't do anything.

Everyone is important in history, because it's about normal people, it's ordinary people as well as all the famous.

Is history harder than maths?

No, in history you've got books to look back on to solve the problem, but in maths you've got to solve the problem yourself.

History is harder than maths. In history you have to be a detective, but in maths you've got laws and they always stay the same. It's easier to solve an equation than to figure out why something happened. You've got more explaining to do in history.

◆ *How much of the citizenship web can you spin?*

You will have used a lot of these citizenship skills from studying *Dying for the Vote*. Which can you spin into the citizenship web? Shade in those skills you have used already on your own copy of the web.

Use four different colours:

- ◆ one for skills you have used in this book
- ◆ one for skills used in other history topics
- ◆ one for skills used in other subjects
- ◆ one for skills you need to develop.

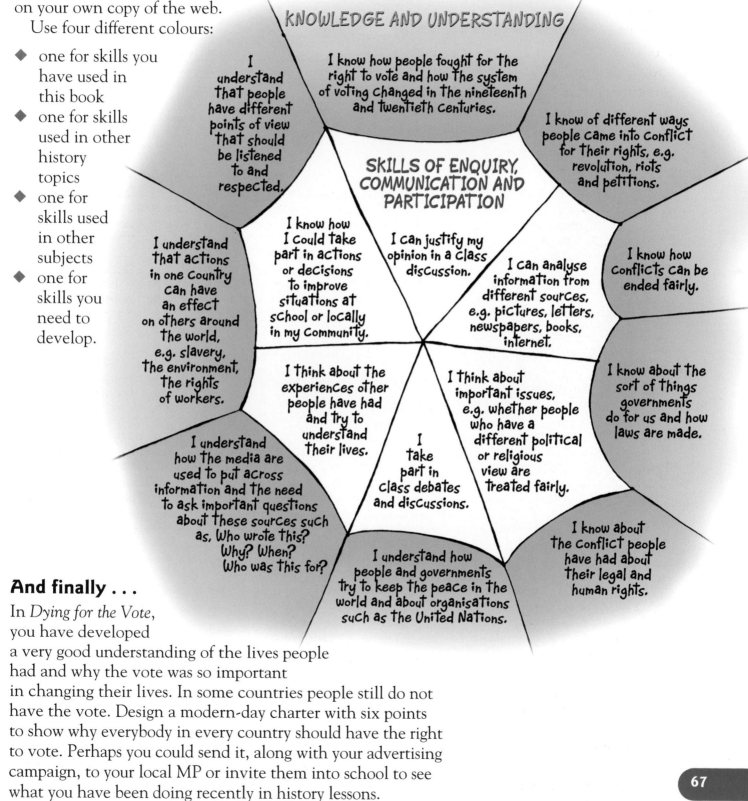

KNOWLEDGE AND UNDERSTANDING

I know how people fought for the right to vote and how the system of voting changed in the nineteenth and twentieth centuries.

I understand that people have different points of view that should be listened to and respected.

I know of different ways people came into conflict for their rights, e.g. revolution, riots and petitions.

SKILLS OF ENQUIRY, COMMUNICATION AND PARTICIPATION

I understand that actions in one country can have an effect on others around the world, e.g. slavery, the environment, the rights of workers.

I know how I could take part in actions or decisions to improve situations at school or locally in my community.

I can justify my opinion in a class discussion.

I can analyse information from different sources, e.g. pictures, letters, newspapers, books, internet.

I know how conflicts can be ended fairly.

I think about the experiences other people have had and try to understand their lives.

I think about important issues, e.g. whether people who have a different political or religious view are treated fairly.

I know about the sort of things governments do for us and how laws are made.

I understand how the media are used to put across information and the need to ask important questions about these sources such as, Who wrote this? Why? When? Who was this for?

I take part in class debates and discussions.

I understand how people and governments try to keep the peace in the world and about organisations such as the United Nations.

I know about the conflict people have had about their legal and human rights.

And finally . . .

In *Dying for the Vote*, you have developed a very good understanding of the lives people had and why the vote was so important in changing their lives. In some countries people still do not have the vote. Design a modern-day charter with six points to show why everybody in every country should have the right to vote. Perhaps you could send it, along with your advertising campaign, to your local MP or invite them into school to see what you have been doing recently in history lessons.

◆ Glossary

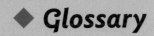

BRIBE	to persuade someone by promising them money or favours
CHARTISM	the movement that campaigned for political reforms in the 1800s. The name comes from the 'People's Charter' that listed the reforms needed. Supporters were known as Chartists
CONSTITUENCY	an area of voters who elect an MP
EXTREMIST	a person who takes violent or extreme action in support of a cause
MILITANT	aggressively active, especially in support of a cause
MUSKET	a lightweight gun, used by soldiers who fought on foot
PETITION	a formal written request appealing to a government, usually signed by many people
PIKE	a weapon made from a long wooden pole with a pointed steel or iron head, used by soldiers who fought on foot
PROPAGANDA	ideas and facts deliberately spread to influence people's opinions
SABRE	a sword with a curved blade, used by soldiers on horseback
SECRET BALLOT	voting in secret by putting a voting paper in a sealed box
SUFFRAGETTES	campaigners for women's suffrage who used violent as well as peaceful methods
SUFFRAGISTS	supporters of women's suffrage who campaigned peacefully
TEXTILE	woven cloth, for example, cotton
TRANSPORTATION	punishing people by sending them to a distant country, for example, from Britain to Australia in the 1800s
VILLEIN	in the Middle Ages, a villager who was not free, for example, to leave the village or to marry without his lord's permission

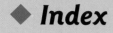

Index

◆ Titles in the series

Pupils' Books (PB) and Teachers' Resource Books (TRB) are available for all titles.

Write Your Own Roman Story	**PB** 0 7195 7717 9	**TRB** 0 7195 7718 7
The Norman Conquest	**PB** 0 7195 8555 4	**TRB** 0 7195 8556 2
King John	**PB** 0 7195 8539 2	**TRB** 0 7195 8540 6
Lost in Time	**PB** 0 7195 8557 0	**TRB** 0 7195 8558 9
'King' Cromwell?	**PB** 0 7195 8559 7	**TRB** 0 7195 8560 0
The Impact of Empire	**PB** 0 7195 8561 9	**TRB** 0 7195 8562 7
Dying for the Vote	**PB** 0 7195 8563 5	**TRB** 0 7195 8564 3
The Trenches	**PB** 0 7195 8565 1	**TRB** 0 7195 8566 X
The Holocaust	**PB** 0 7195 7709 8	**TRB** 0 7195 7710 1
The Twentieth Century	**PB** 0 7195 7711 X	**TRB** 0 7195 7712 8

◆ Acknowledgements

Photographs reproduced by kind permission of:
Cover by permission of People's History Museum; **p.8** *all* Mary Evans Picture Library; **p.14** Art Archive; **p.16** Hulton Archive; **p.26/7** Royal Archives © HM Queen Elizabeth II; **p.27** People's History Museum; **p.36/7** Museum of London; **p.38** Tate, London 2002; **p.40** *all* Mary Evans Picture Library; **p.41** Mary Evans Picture Library; **p.42** *all* Museum of London; **p.43** *all* Museum of London; **p.44** *tl* Popperfoto, *tr, bl* Museum of London; **p.45** *all* Museum of London; **p.46** *all* Museum of London; **p.47** *tl, bl* Museum of London, *tr* Mary Evans Picture Library; **p.48** Museum of London; **p.49** *tl* Museum of London, *tr* Hulton Archive, *bl* National Portrait Gallery; **p.51** *tl* Mary Evans Picture Library, *tr, bl* Museum of London; **p.52** British Library Newspaper Archives; **p.53** *l* Mary Evans Picture Library, *r* Centre for Study of Cartoons & Caricatures, University of Kent/Mirror Syndication; **p.54** *t* Museum of London; *b* Imperial War Museum; **p.55** *all* Imperial War Museum; **p.60** Associated Press; **p.61** Imperial War Museum; **p.64** *tr* British Library, *bl* Hulton Archive; **p.65** *all* Museum of London.

(*t* = top, *b* = bottom, *l* = left, *r* = right, *c* = centre)

While every effort has been made to contact copyright holders, the Publishers apologise for any omissions, which they will be pleased to rectify at the earliest opportunity.